# Introducción a los padres

**We Both Read** es la primera serie de libros diseñada para invitar a padres e hijos a compartir la lectura de un cuento, por turnos y en voz alta. Esta "lectura compartida"—que se ha desarrollado en conjunto con especialistas en primeras lecturas—invita a los padres a leer los textos más complejos en la página de la izquierda. Luego, les toca a los niños leer las páginas de la derecha, que contienen textos más sencillos, escritos específicamente para primeros lectores.

Leer en voz alta es una de las actividades más importantes que los padres comparten con sus hijos para ayudarlos a desarrollar la lectura. Sin embargo, We Both Read no es solo leerle *a* un niño, sino que les permite a los padres leer *con* el niño. We Both Read es más poderoso y efectivo porque combina dos elementos claves del aprendizaje: "demostración" (el padre lee) y "aplicación" (el niño lee). El resultado no es solo que el niño aprende a leer más rápido, ¡sino que ambos disfrutan y se enriquecen con esta experiencia!

Sería más útil si usted lee el libro completo y en voz alta la primera vez, y luego invita a su niño a participar en una segunda lectura. En algunos libros, las palabras más difíciles se presentan por primera vez en **negritas** en el texto del padre. Señalar o hablar sobre estas palabras ayudará a su niño a familiarizarse con ellas y a ampliar su vocabulario. También notará que el ícono "lee el padre" ⊙ precede el texto del padre y el ícono "lee el niño" ⊙ precede el texto del niño.

Lo invitamos a compartir y a relacionarse con su niño mientras leen el libro juntos. Si su hijo tiene dificultad, usted puede mencionar algunas cosas que lo ayuden. "Decir cada sonido" es bueno, pero puede que esto no funcione con todas las palabras. Los niños pueden hallar pistas en las palabras del cuento, en el contexto de las oraciones e incluso en las imágenes. Algunos cuentos incluyen patrones y rimas que los ayudarán. También le podría ser útil a su niño tocar las palabras con su dedo mientras lee, para conectar mejor el sonido de la voz con la palabra impresa.

¡Al compartir los libros de We Both Read, usted y su hijo vivirán juntos la fascinante aventura de la lectura! Es una manera divertida y fácil de animar y ayudar a su niño a leer—¡y una maravillosa manera de preparar a su niño para disfrutar de la lectura durante toda su vida!

## Parent's Introduction

**We Both Read** is the first series of books designed to invite parents and children to share the reading of a story by taking turns reading aloud. This "shared reading" innovation, which was developed with reading education specialists, invites parents to read the more complex text and story line on the left-hand pages. Then, children can be encouraged to read the right-hand pages, which feature text written for a specific early reading level.

Reading aloud is one of the most important activities parents can share with their child to assist them in their reading development. However, We Both Read goes beyond reading *to* a child and allows parents to share the reading *with* a child. We Both Read is so powerful and effective because it combines two key elements in learning: "modeling" (the parent reads) and "doing" (the child reads). The result is not only faster reading development for the child, but a much more enjoyable and enriching experience for both!

You may find it helpful to read the entire book aloud yourself the first time, then invite your child to participate in the second reading. In some books, a few more difficult words will first be introduced in the parent's text, distinguished with bold lettering. Pointing out, and even discussing, these words will help familiarize your child with them and help to build your child's vocabulary. Also, note that a "talking parent" icon ⊙ precedes the parent's text, and a "talking child" icon ⊙ precedes the child's text.

We encourage you to share and interact with your child as you read the book together. If your child is having difficulty, you might want to mention a few things to help him. "Sounding out" is good, but it will not work with all words. Children can pick up clues about the words they are reading from the story, the context of the sentence, or even the pictures. Some stories have rhyming patterns that might help. It might also help them to touch the words with their finger as they read, to better connect the voice sound and the printed word.

Sharing the We Both Read books together will engage you and your child in an interactive adventure in reading! It is a fun and easy way to encourage and help your child to read—and a wonderful way to start them off on a lifetime of reading enjoyment!

**About Bugs / Acerca de los insectos**
Second Edition
A Bilingual We Both Read Book
Level 2

———————————————————————————————

Use of photographs provided by iStock, Dreamstime, Dr. Edward Ross
and Animals Animals/Richard Kolar, Patti Murray, Donald Specker,
Ken G. Preston-Mafham, Michael Fogden, James H. Robinson,
Stephen Dalton, Michael Andrews,Doug Wechsler, G. I. Bernard, O. S. F.,
Raymond A. Mendez, Bruce Davidson, Richard La Val.
Translation Services by Cambridge BrickHouse, Inc.
Bilingual adaptation © 2016 by Treasure Bay, Inc.

We Both Read® is a trademark of Treasure Bay, Inc.

Published by Treasure Bay, Inc.
P.O. Box 119
Novato, CA 94948 USA

Printed in Malaysia

Library of Congress Catalog Card Number: 2016945522

Paperback ISBN: 978-1-60115-084-4

Visit us online at: www.WeBothRead.com

PR-11-16

# WE BOTH READ®

# About Bugs
## *Acerca de los insectos*

Second Edition • Segunda edición

By Sheryl Scarborough

Translated by Yanitzia Canetti

TREASURE BAY

*Ladybug swarm • Enjambre de mariquitas*

Does it sometimes seem like bugs are everywhere? Well, they *are*! There are more bugs, or **insects**, in the world than there are people and all other animals combined. And different kinds of bugs can live in almost any weather condition, from extreme heat to freezing cold. But just what is a bug?

¿No parece a veces que hay insectos por todas partes? Bueno, ¡pues *sí*! Hay más bichitos, o **insectos**, en el mundo, que personas y todos los demás animales combinados. Y los diferentes tipos de insectos pueden vivir en casi cualquier condición climática, desde el calor extremo hasta el frío congelante. Pero en realidad, ¿qué es un insecto?

Head • Cabeza
Thorax • Tórax
Abdomen • Abdomen

*Red ant • Hormiga roja*

The proper name for a bug is "**insect**."
The body of an insect has three parts.
All insects have six legs.
Spiders are *not* insects.
Spiders have eight legs.

El nombre apropiado para un bichito es "**insecto**".
El cuerpo de un insecto tiene tres partes.
Todos los insectos tienen seis patas.
Las arañas *no* son insectos.
Las arañas tienen ocho patas.

*Giraffe beetle (or weevil) • Escarabajo jirafa (o gorgojo)*

One kind of insect is the **beetle**. There are over 500,000 species of **beetle**, each with its own distinct characteristics. The bombardier **beetle**, for example, can shoot an attacking predator with a cloud of foul-smelling hot gas. The **beetle** shown above is called the *giraffe beetle*. Can you guess why?

Una clase de insecto es el **escarabajo**. Hay más de 500 000 clases de **escarabajos**, cada uno con sus propias características. El **escarabajo** bombardero, por ejemplo, puede dispararle una nube de gas mal oliente y caliente a un depredador que lo ataca. El **escarabajo** que se muestra arriba se llama **escarabajo** *jirafa*. ¿Puedes adivinar por qué?

*Rhinoceros beetle • Escarabajo rinoceronte*

**Beetles** come in all shapes and sizes.
Some beetles are good. They eat other bugs.
Some beetles are bad. They eat plants and trees.
Some even eat the rugs in our homes!

Hay **escarabajos** de muchas formas y tamaños.
Algunos escarabajos son buenos. Se comen a otros
insectos. Otros escarabajos son malos. Se comen las
plantas y los árboles. Algunos, incluso, ¡se comen las
alfombras en nuestros hogares!

Stinger • *Aguijón*

*Honeybee with stinger extended • Abeja con su aguijón extendido*

Every **honeybee** hive has one queen that is in charge of the hive and will produce all the offspring. Each spring she sends her workers out to gather **pollen** and **nectar**. The bees then convert the **nectar** into honey, which will be stored for food. Worker bees use their stingers to protect the hive's honey from other animals.

Cada colmena de **abejas** tiene una reina que se encarga de la colmena y de producir toda la descendencia. Cada primavera ella envía a sus obreras a recoger el **polen** y el **néctar**. Luego, las abejas convierten el néctar en miel, que será almacenada como alimento. Las obreras utilizan sus aguijones para proteger la miel de la colmena de los demás animales.

Pollen • Polen

*Honeybee gathering nectar and pollen • Abeja recogiendo néctar y polen*

The **honeybees** gather **pollen** and **nectar** from flowers.
They gather the pollen with their back legs.
Then they fly back to the hive with this food.

Las **abejas** recogen el **polen** y el **néctar** de las flores.
Ellas reúnen el polen con sus patas traseras.
Luego, regresan a la colmena con ese alimento.

*Praying mantis • Mantis religiosa*

**Mantids** are often called *praying mantises* because the position of their front legs gives the impression they are praying. **Mantids** have a huge appetite and eat just about any bug they can grab with their trap-like front legs. They sit very still until another insect approaches, then grab it and eat it alive!

Las **mantis** son a menudo llamadas *mantises religiosas* debido a que la posición de sus patas delanteras dan la impresión de que están orando. Las **mantis** tienen un gran apetito y se comen cualquier insecto que puedan atrapar con sus patas delanteras en forma de trampa. Se quedan muy quietas hasta que otro insecto se les acerca, ¡entonces lo atrapan y se lo comen vivo!

*Leaf-like mantid • Mantis tipo hoja*

There are many kinds of **mantids**.
Some are hard to see when they are on a plant.
This helps mantids hide from animals that eat bugs.
This one looks like a leaf.

Hay muchos tipos de **mantis**.
Algunas son difíciles de ver cuando están en una planta.
Esto ayuda a las mantis a esconderse de los animales
que se alimentan de insectos. Esta se ve como una hoja.

9

*Giant weta • Weta gigante*

The New Zealand **weta**, which is close to extinction, lives on protected islands near New Zealand. This is one of the largest known insects and can weigh as much as a small bird. Its scientific name, *Deinacrida*, means "demon grasshopper" because it looks like a large, armor-plated grasshopper.

El **weta** de Nueva Zelanda, que está casi en extinción, vive en islas protegidas cerca de Nueva Zelanda. Este es uno de los insectos más grandes conocidos y pueden pesar tanto como un pequeño pájaro. Su nombre científico, *Deinacrida*, significa "saltamontes demonio" porque parece un saltamontes grande, blindado.

*Wellington tree weta • Weta de los árboles de Wellington*

The **weta** lives in a hole in the ground.
It only comes out at night.
The weta's ears are on its legs.
Can you find them?


El **weta** vive en un agujero en el suelo.
Solo sale de noche.
Los oídos del weta están en sus patas.
¿Puedes encontrarlos?

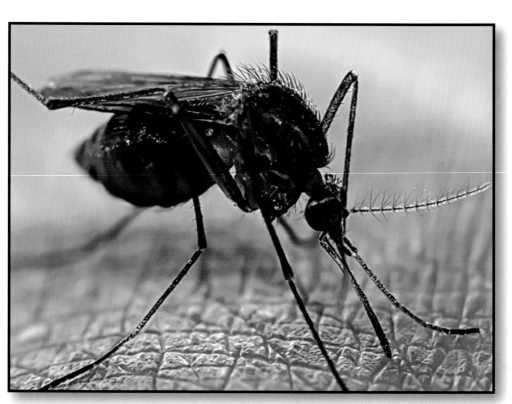

*Mosquito • Mosquito*

**Mosquitoes** are often called the vampires of the bug world. Female **mosquitoes** (the only ones that "bite") actually pierce your skin with a tube-like mouthpart called a *stylet*. First they inject saliva, and then suck blood through the same *stylet*. It's the saliva that makes you itch!

Los **mosquitos** son llamados con frecuencia los vampiros del mundo de los insectos. Los **mosquitos** hembras (los únicos que "pican") en realidad perforan tu piel con un aparato bucal en forma de tubo llamado *estilete*. Primero inyectan saliva y después chupan la sangre por el mismo *estilete*. ¡Es la saliva la que te pica!

*Mosquito larvae and pupa • Larvas y crisálidas de mosquito*

**Mosquitoes** lay their eggs in standing water.
Young mosquitoes find food in the water.
They will stay near water until they are
old enough to fly away.

Los **mosquitos** ponen sus huevos en el agua estancada.
Los mosquitos jóvenes encuentran alimento en el agua.
Ellos se quedan cerca del agua hasta alcanzar la edad
suficiente para volar lejos.

*Rabbit flea on rabbit ear • Pulga de conejo en la oreja del conejo*

Another blood-sucking member of the insect world is the **flea**. These tiny bugs are only about the size of a pinhead, but they can deliver a very big "itch"! The small, flat, slippery body of the **flea** allows it to slide easily through the hairs or feathers of its involuntary "host."

Otro miembro chupador de sangre del mundo de los insectos es la **pulga**. Estos pequeños insectos son solo del tamaño de la cabeza de un alfiler, pero pueden provocar ¡una gran "picazón"! El cuerpo pequeño, plano y resbaladizo de la **pulga** le permite deslizarse fácilmente entre los pelos o las plumas de su "huésped" involuntario.

*Cat flea jumping • Pulga de gato saltando*

A **flea** has strong back legs that help it jump.
A flea can jump very high.
It can jump from the ground up to your knees.
That's a big jump for a little flea!

La **pulga** tiene unas fuertes patas traseras que le ayudan
a saltar. Una pulga puede saltar muy alto.
Ella puede saltar desde el suelo hasta tus rodillas.
¡Eso es un salto muy grande para una pulga tan pequeña!

*Monarch butterfly • Mariposa monarca*

Insects can look strange, but they can also be quite beautiful. Butterflies are some of the most beautiful insects. There are thousands of kinds of butterflies, but they all go through four stages in their life cycles. Each starts as an egg, hatches into a **caterpillar**, then encases itself in a chrysalis (KRIS-a-lis) before finally emerging as a butterfly.

Los insectos pueden ser extraños, pero también pueden ser muy hermosos. Las mariposas son unos de los insectos más bellos. Existen miles de tipos de mariposas, pero todos pasan por cuatro etapas en su ciclo biológico. Todos comienzan como un huevo, salen del cascarón como una **oruga**, luego se encierran en una crisálida antes de emerger finalmente como una mariposa.

*Moth caterpillar shedding skin • Oruga de polilla mudando la piel*

A **caterpillar's** job is to eat and grow.
Its skin does not grow with it.
It breaks open when it gets too tight.
Then the caterpillar crawls out in a new soft skin.

El trabajo de una **oruga** es comer y crecer.
Su piel no crece con ella.
Se rompe y se abre cuando se pone demasiado apretada.
Luego, la oruga se escurre fuera en su nueva y suave piel.

17

*Monarch caterpillar forming chrysalis • Orugas monarcas formando crisálidas.*

After about two weeks of eating and growing, a monarch caterpillar creates a hard **chrysalis** around itself. The **chrysalis** may be found suspended from a branch where its coloring will blend in to protect it from predators. Inside the **chrysalis**, amazing things are happening. The caterpillar is transforming from a wiggly worm-like creature into a full-grown butterfly.

Después de unas dos semanas de comer y crecer, la oruga monarca crea una dura **crisálida** a su alrededor. Las **crisálidas** pueden encontrarse suspendidas de una rama donde su coloración se confunde con esta, para protegerse de los depredadores. Dentro de la **crisálida** están sucediendo cosas increíbles. La oruga se está transformando de una criatura con forma de gusano en una hermosa mariposa completamente adulta.

*Monarch butterfly emerging from chrysalis • Mariposa monarca saliendo de la crisálida*

Breaking out of the **chrysalis** is hard work. When it finally gets out, a butterfly's wings are folded and damp. It must flap them to pump blood into them. Then the butterfly can fly away.

Romper la **crisálida** es un trabajo duro. Cuando finalmente logra salir, las alas de la mariposa están pegadas y húmedas. Tiene que aletear fuerte para bombear la sangre hacia ellas. Entonces la mariposa puede volar.

*Honey pot ants • Hormigas mieleras*

There are over 8,000 different kinds, or *species*, of ants, each with its own fascinating method of survival. Some are fierce hunters. Others harvest and store seeds. Honey pot ants use some of the ants in their **colony** as living storage containers to hold sweet juice for the winter or a dry season. Another interesting type of ant is the **leafcutter** ant.

Hay más de 8000 tipos diferentes, o *especies*, de hormigas, cada una con su propio método de supervivencia fascinante. Algunas son feroces cazadoras. Otras cosechan y almacenan semillas. Las hormigas mieleras utilizan a algunas hormigas de su **colonia** como recipientes vivientes para guardar el dulce jugo para el invierno o una estación seca. Otro tipo interesante de hormiga es la hormiga **corta hojas**.

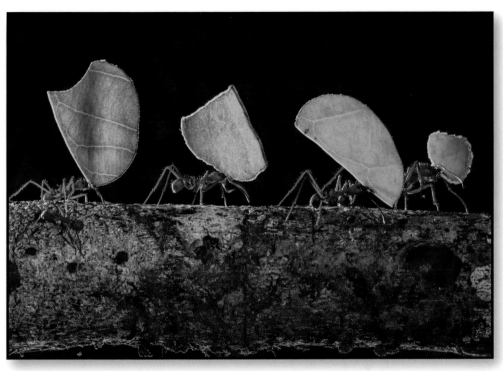

*Leaf cutter ants • Hormigas corta hojas*

**Leafcutter** ants use their jaws to cut leaves into tiny pieces. Then they carry the pieces back to their nest. A **colony** of leafcutter ants can cut all the leaves off of a tree in just one day!

Las hormigas **corta hojas** utilizan sus mandíbulas para cortar las hojas en trozos pequeños. Luego se llevan los pedazos a su nido. Una **colonia** de hormigas corta hojas puede cortar todas las hojas de un árbol ¡en un solo día!

*Tarantula hawk wasp and tarantula • Avispa caza tarántula y tarántula*

The tarantula hawk **wasp** is one of the most fascinating species in the **wasp** family. This **wasp** will inject a tarantula spider with a paralyzing venom, then lay a single egg on its warm, furry back. The **wasp's** resulting larva then feeds on the immobilized spider until it's strong enough to be on its own.

La **avispa** caza tarántula es una de las especies más fascinantes de la familia de las **avispas**. Esta **avispa** inyecta a una tarántula con un veneno paralizante, luego pone un solo huevo en su cálida y peluda espalda. La larva de **avispa** que nace entonces se alimenta de la araña inmovilizada, hasta que es suficientemente fuerte para sobrevivir por sí misma.

*Social wasps on a nest • Avispas sociales en su nido*

There are many different kinds of **wasps**.
Some wasps make paper to build their nests.
People may have learned how to make paper
by watching these wasps.

Hay muchos tipos de **avispas**.
Algunas avispas hacen papel para construir sus
nidos. Puede que las personas hayan aprendido a
hacer papel observando estas avispas.

23

*Assassin bug piercing grasshopper head • Un insecto asesino perfora la cabeza de un saltamontes.*

**Assassin** bugs are some of the insect world's most impressive predators, and each of the hundreds of species hunt, kill, and feed in a similar way. Most wait quietly in hiding to surprise their victim, then use their dagger-like beak to kill their prey. This same beak also serves as a feeding tube for the **assassin** bug.

Los insectos **asesinos** son algunos de los depredadores más impresionantes del mundo de los insectos, y cada uno de los cientos de especies que existen cazan, matan y se alimentan de manera similar. La mayoría espera en silencio, escondidos, para sorprender a su víctima, luego utilizan su pico en forma de daga para matar a sus presas. Este mismo pico también sirve como tubo de alimentación para el insecto **asesino**.

*Assassin bug nymph • Ninfa de insecto asesino*

Some **assassin** bugs live near people and may bite them. It hurts when an assassin bug bites, but the bite does not kill people.

Algunos insectos **asesinos** viven cerca de la gente y podrían picarlos. Cuando un insecto asesino pica, duele, pero su picadura no mata a las personas.

*American cockroach head • Cabeza de cucaracha americana*

Many people think **cockroaches** are nasty, dirty creatures, but these bugs actually clean themselves as often as cats. **Cockroaches** roamed Earth before the dinosaurs and are so adaptable to their environment they will probably continue to roam for a long time to come.

Mucha gente piensa que las **cucarachas** son criaturas repugnantes y sucias, sin embargo, estos insectos se limpian con la misma frecuencia que los gatos. Las **cucarachas** vagaban por la Tierra antes que los dinosaurios y son tan adaptables a su entorno que probablemente continuarán su vagar durante mucho tiempo en el futuro.

*Giant cockroach • Cucaracha gigante*

A **cockroach** can be as small as an ant.
Some can be as big as a mouse.
This one is called a giant cave cockroach.
It can grow to be almost four inches long!

Una **cucaracha** puede ser tan pequeña como una hormiga.
Algunas pueden ser tan grandes como un ratón.
Esta se llama cucaracha gigante de cueva.
¡Ella puede crecer hasta tener casi cuatro pulgadas de largo!

*Southern* Aeshna *dragonfly* • *Libélula* Aeshna *del Sur*

The wings of the brightly colored **dragonfly** seem fragile but are actually such powerful and efficient flight organs that the US military studied them to try and make their planes fly faster. A **dragonfly's** head is almost all eye. This allows **dragonflies** to see prey up to forty feet away.

Las brillantes y coloreadas alas de la **libélula** parecen frágiles, pero son en realidad unos órganos de vuelo tan potentes y eficientes, que el ejército estadounidense los estudió para tratar de hacer que sus aviones volaran más rápido. La cabeza de una **libélula** es ojo casi toda. Esto le permite a las **libélulas** ver a sus presas hasta cuarenta pies de distancia.

*Red dragonfly on sisal leaf • Libélula roja en una hoja de pita*

**Dragonflies** have been on Earth a long time. They were on Earth before the dinosaurs. Back then a dragonfly was longer than your arm. Now a dragonfly can be about as long as your hand.

Las **libélulas** han habitado la Tierra desde hace mucho tiempo. Estaban en la Tierra antes que los dinosaurios. En aquel entonces, una libélula era más larga que tu brazo. Ahora una libélula solo puede ser del largo de tu mano.

29

Fulgora *(lantern bug) head* • *Cabeza del* Fulgora *(insecto linterna)*

This odd looking bug with a head shaped like a peanut is found in the tropical regions of Central and South America. It goes by many names including **lantern** *bug*, *peanut bug*, and *alligator bug*. Its "peanut head" is a form of protection, making it look like a lizard to an attacking **enemy**.

Este insecto de aspecto extraño, con cabeza en forma de maní, se encuentra en las regiones tropicales de América Central y del Sur. Se le conoce por muchos nombres, entre ellos: *insecto* **linterna**, *insecto maní*, e *insecto cocodrilo*. Su "cabeza de maní" es una forma de protección, pues hace que se vea como un lagarto ante un **enemigo** atacante.

Fulgora *(lantern bug) with wings extended* • Fulgora *(insecto linterna) con sus alas extendidas*

**Lantern** bugs spread their wings when an **enemy** comes near. Spots on its wings look like the eyes of an owl. This is another way to scare away an enemy.

Los insectos **linterna** extienden sus alas cuando un **enemigo** se les acerca. Las manchas en las alas se parecen a los ojos de un búho. Esta es otra manera de ahuyentar a un enemigo.

*Walking stick • Insecto bastón*

**Walking sticks** are insects that look just like the twigs of the trees in which they live. This natural camouflage makes them appear to be something inedible to birds, their main enemies. **Walking sticks** are hungry leaf-eating vegetarians that do most of their eating at night when the birds are asleep.

Los **bastones** son insectos que se parecen a las ramas de los árboles en que viven. Este camuflaje natural hace que parezcan no comestibles para las aves, sus principales enemigos. Los **bastones** son vegetarianos, son ávidos comedores de hojas y toman la mayor parte de su alimento por la noche, cuando las aves están dormidas.

*Dead leaf butterfly • Mariposa hoja seca*

A **walking stick** stays safe by not being seen.
Many bugs stay safe this way.
This butterfly looks like a dead leaf.


El **bastón** se mantiene a salvo porque no lo ven.
Muchos insectos se mantienen a salvo de esta manera.
Esta mariposa se parece a una hoja muerta.

*Queen, worker, and soldier termites • Termitas reina, obreras y guerreras*

**Termites** are little bugs that eat wood at an amazing rate and can cause lots of damage to houses. **Termite** colonies have a queen that lays all the eggs and is cared for by the worker **termites**. In some parts of the world, certain types of **termites** build huge **mounds**.

Las **termitas** son pequeños insectos que se alimentan de la madera a un ritmo increíble, y pueden causar mucho daño a las casas. Las colonias de **termitas** tienen una reina que pone todos los huevos y es cuidada por las **termitas** obreras. En algunas partes del mundo, ciertos tipos de **termitas** construyen enormes **montículos**.

*Gigantic termite nest • Nido de termitas gigante*

**Termite mounds** are also called nests. They are full of tunnels to let in air. They also have rooms for storing food. Some termite mounds can be taller than a person!

Los **montículos** de **termitas** son también llamados nidos. Están llenos de túneles que dejan entrar el aire. También tienen zonas para almacenar alimentos. Algunos montículos de termitas ¡pueden ser más altos que una persona!

*Fork-tailed bush katydid • Katydid cola de tenedor*

*Katy-did-katy-did!* That's the beautiful love call of the **katydid**. **Katydids** make their distinctive sounds, often called their "song," by rubbing the base of their front wings together. Many start their song at twilight and sing through the entire night, hoping to attract a mate.

*¡Shi-shi-shi-shi-shi-shi!* Ese es el hermoso llamado de amor del **katydid**. Los **katydids** hacen su peculiar sonido, a menudo llamado su "canto", frotando la base de las alas delanteras entre sí. Muchos comienzan su canto en el crepúsculo y cantan durante toda la noche con la esperanza de atraer a su pareja.

*Spike-headed katydid • Katydid cabeza de púa*

This is a spike-headed **katydid**. It lives in South America. Some kinds of katydids eat snails, frogs' eggs, and other insects. A spike-headed katydid only eats plants.

Este es un **katydid** cabeza de púa. Él vive en América del Sur. Algunos tipos de katydids comen caracoles, huevos de rana y otros insectos. Un katydid cabeza de púa se alimenta solo de plantas.

*Goliath beetle • Escarabajo goliat*

There are over one million known species of bugs in the world. Here are some fun facts about some of them. One of the smallest known insects is the hummingbird flower mite. It lives in the nose of a hummingbird! One of the heaviest flying insects is the five-inch-long, massively armored goliath beetle of Africa.

Se conoce más de un millón de especies de insectos en el mundo. Estos son algunos datos curiosos sobre algunos de ellos. Uno de los insectos más pequeños conocidos es el ácaro del colibrí de las flores. ¡Vive en la nariz de un colibrí! Uno de los insectos voladores más pesados es el escarabajo goliat, de África, con cinco pulgadas de largo y completamente blindado.

*Hawk moth • Polilla halcón*

One of the fastest running bugs is the cockroach.
It can run sixty feet per minute.
One of the fastest flying bugs is the hawk moth.
It can fly up to thirty-three miles per hour.


Uno de los insectos que corre más rápido es la cucaracha.
Puede correr sesenta pies por minuto.
Uno de los insectos voladores más rápidos es la polilla halcón.
Puede alcanzar hasta treinta y tres millas por hora.

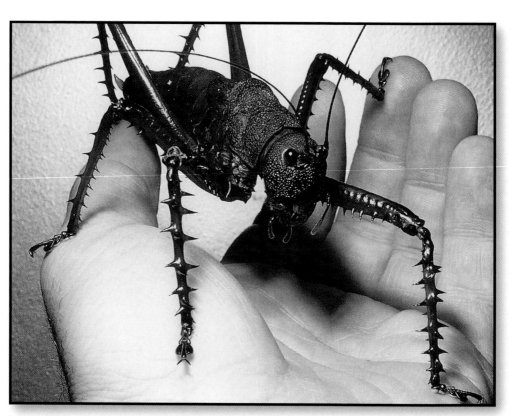

*Weta-like katydid • Katydid tipo weta*

Insects appear in an amazing variety of shapes, sizes, and colors. Some have no ears or noses on their faces yet can smell and hear better than humans. Some have two wings, some have four, and some have no wings at all. People called *entomologists* spend their lives studying these fascinating creatures we call bugs.

Los insectos tienen una sorprendente variedad de formas, tamaños y colores. Algunos no tienen oídos o nariz en sus caras, pero pueden oler y oír mejor que los humanos. Unos tienen dos alas, otros tienen cuatro, y algunos no tienen ninguna. Los *entomólogos* se pasan la vida estudiando estas fascinantes criaturas que llamamos insectos.

*Scarab taking flight • Escarabajo iniciando vuelo*

Would you like to study bugs?
You can start in your own yard!
Bugs are everywhere.
How many different kinds can you find?


¿Te gustaría estudiar los insectos?
¡Puedes comenzar en tu propio patio!
Los insectos están en todas partes.
¿Cuántos tipos diferentes puedes encontrar?

If you liked **About Bugs**, here is another
We Both Read® book you are sure to enjoy!

*Si te gustó **Acerca de los insectos**, ¡seguramente disfrutarás
este otro libro de la serie We Both Read®!*

### Endangered Animals • Animales en peligro de extinción

This book takes a close look at various animals from around the world that are in danger of becoming extinct. It discusses how the animals have become endangered due to worldwide threats including pollution, deforestation, and global warming. Featuring stunning photographs of many endangered animals in their natural habitats, the book also relates some of the positive steps being taken to protect the animals and explains how we can all take part in saving them.

*Este libro examina en detalle varios animales del mundo que están en peligro de extinción. Se analiza cómo los animales pasaron a estar en peligro de extinción debido a las amenazas en todo el mundo, incluida la contaminación, la deforestación y el calentamiento global. Con fotografías de muchos animales en peligro de extinción en su hábitat natural, el libro también se refiere a algunas de las medidas que se están adoptando para proteger a los animales y explica cómo todos podemos hacer algo para salvarlos.*

To see all the We Both Read books that are available,
just go online to **www.WeBothRead.com**.

*Para ver todos los libros disponibles de la serie We Both Read®,
visita nuestra página web: **www.TreasureBayBooks.com***